Dear Friends,

     I am honored and privileged to present you with this copy of *The Bondage of Bitterness*. My prayer for anyone who reads this book is that it will provide enlightenment during a season of darkness, hope in the midst of a trial, and encouragement during times of despair.

     There are many times in life where we find ourselves engulfed by life's problems. These times causes us to be weighed down with doubt, worry, and fear. This message is a reminder that you response matters. It is always better to allow God to do the heavy lifting during moments of ambiguity.

     I want you to know that my prayers and thoughts are with you. May this book serve as a compass while you seek God's direction for your life.

In His Service,

Mervin W. January

Mervin W. January

ALSO BY MERVIN JANUARY

How to catch a "falling" Marriage

(Secrets of Marriage, Love, & Relationships are revealed)

God's Secret Sauce

(A 40-day devotional to reinforce your faith)

"The Bondage of Bitterness"

(A how-to guide in the Art of Forgiving)

An inspirational novel by: Mervin W. January

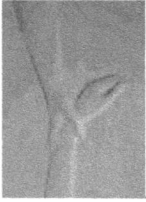

Against All Odds Publishing

DEDICATION:

All proceeds from this message are dedicated to continue winning souls for the Kingdom of God. Also, an exclusive dedication to Alexandria, Jonathan, Mae-Gayle, and Milan! But, of course, the ULTIMATE dedication belongs to my wife Monique. She is my favor from God.

Prologue

INTRODUCTION

God is the source of our strength. He has a way of training us to trust in Him through the trials of life. Although we are saved, many of our minds are in turmoil. We come to God with our baggage. We have been abused physically, mentally, sexually, and financially. We are victims of injustice, mistreatment, and abuse. In the midst of it all, forgiveness covers our heart and other extremities. Why is it so important? Un-forgiveness rarely hurts the other person; yet, it always hurts you. Also, God said that He will not forgive you unless you forgive others. Your decision to walk in love is what will activate God's forgiveness when you need it. It is the trigger that enables you to decide that their wrong will not affect the decision you have made. Love is the key that unlocks forgiveness for you.

The church is more than a mere place of worship. It is designed to be a safe haven for wounded souls. Although it may help us to deal with sin, it does not always help us to deal with being sinned against by others. There are generally three classes of people including Predators, Victims, and Victimized Predators. Predators inflict their will on others. Victims innocently receive the negative impact from the force of the predator. Finally, the Victimized Predator longs to do to others what was done to them. This is a result of fleshly thinking. Our flesh is much more powerful than we think. It can become an almost untamable beast. It took me years to simply understand the power of fleshly thinking. I am finally on the road to recovery.

As Christians, we label the rough times as a wilderness experience. This is a place that lacks maturity and the irrigation of God's word. It tends to resist opportunities for growth. It causes painful memories to flow through our mind like tumbleweeds in a desert. Here we must surrender our will to the Father. It is only then that God can take us from salvation to liberation (total freedom). But in order to complete this process, we have to be transformed by the renewing of our minds. Understanding the process helps us to achieve the purpose. We have to get to a place where growth is not trading places with our predators. This is a position where we no longer see ourselves as victims. From this posture, revenge is no longer an option. What you do in the hard times will determine what you really believe. You see, anybody can believe all kinds of stuff sitting in the church or when all is right in our lives. But it is the hard time that causes us to find out who we really are.

We know some things about ourselves that make us feel as though we are ineligible for the promises of God. Familiar memories of painful experiences can be fatal. Sometimes we see ourselves as being what we went through. Rather than understanding that we can go through it and not become it. This is an inspiring story of liberation. We learn to trust in God through days of heartbreak, loneliness, and rejection. He teaches us how to develop an appetite for righteousness. His peace bathes our soul in tranquility. The goodness of God comforts us. God's engrafted word really does work for us. He strengthens us through His word. He takes us from faith to faith so that He can get some glory out of our story. Life is the class; showing unconditional love is the lesson.

CHAPTER 1: This is who I am

Zechariah 4:10

[10] Who [with reason] despises the day of small things (beginnings)?
(AMP)

I was born in the scanty confines of Winnsboro, Louisiana. Our house was located in a neighborhood that seemed to be in the middle of nowhere across the street from nothing. I grew up learning about farm animals, harvesting cotton, lawn maintenance, small-town life, easy country living, and watching my mother love her enemies because Jesus died for our sins. My fondest childhood memories consisted of catching crayfish, mud-crawling after a flood, sandlot football, little league baseball, singing in the church choir, two years of high school football and playing in the marching band. I hit numerous home-runs in little league. The only catch is that many of our parks did not have an outfield fence, but they still counted as homers because of how far I could hit the ball. Of course, the older I got the better I was☺. I had an extremely small circle of friends. The four of us were knit closely together by parents who worked long hours and the usual boredom of growing up in the rural south. The common bond that we all shared was growing up in a household of multiple surnames. All of our parents had experienced at least one divorce.

We started a clubhouse called the Apaches. Dues were only $0.25 per week. We finally saved enough to have a little party. There was kool-aid, cookies, and chips. The feeling of accomplishment provided a nice emotional rush! Thanks to peer pressure, my virginity became a thing of the past by age 16. During my final two years of high school, I mowed lawns and chopped cotton over the summer for extra money. Deep within the recesses of my heart, I always envisioned myself with great wealth. We may have been poor, but I was plenty happy during my childhood.

Our family went to bible class each Wednesday and church every Sunday. Attendance was NOT AN OPTION! We were there with bells on, even when none of the other members would show up. My mother was smart enough to know that God is the only true source of joy. She made sure that the foundation according to Jesus Christ was fully established in our hearts. We were on the welfare system for a while, but later, my mother got enough education to become a licensed nurse. It seems that we were moving on up like *George & Weezy* of The Jeffersons TV Show ever since.

I grew up the youngest of 4 children that included a brother and two sisters. My older siblings usually always had some sort of job. They bagged groceries, chopped cotton, picked potatoes, picked cotton, babysat, and more. The younger of my two sisters was what we called a "Miss Goodie Too Shoes." She seemed to receive a little more favoritism than the rest of us. I cannot remember her ever having a grade point average less than 3.7 out a 4.0 grading system. She was a track and basketball star from junior high school until well into her final college years. I felt like my mother would always compare us to one another. To this day, I believe that it was unintentional. Yet, I distinctively remember lashing out against my mother as a teenager saying, "Stop comparing us to one another, we are two different people." Growing up, I was always her little brother. I wanted my own identity. It seemed as a teenager that the spirit of rebellion was born out of this feeling. This is when I knew that I would leave the small confines of this hick town never to return, except to visit. I clearly remember wanting a pair of Nike tennis shoes so bad that it left an unpleasant taste in my mouth. Yet, I always knew that my mother could not afford to give us certain wants as children. I finally accepted the fact that Adidas were not so bad. I learned to take comfort in the fact that I could make "no name" clothes look good.

My grandfather was the only father that I ever truly knew. His 6'3" 290+ pound frame was something to behold. When he stood up in the room, he looked like a big tall tree. He had big hands, big feet, stocky, and a nice haircut. He raised chickens, geese, and hogs for profit. He spent all of his time churching, working, fixing, and providing. He repeatedly quoted bible verses and attended area churches on behalf of our church congregation. While attending different programs, it was customary that someone would come and represent from each church on the program. We would sing songs affectionately referred to as "Dr. Watts" or old Negro spirituals without structured music or time signatures. I spent the first eight years of my life with him learning about life. He only whipped me once during my entire life. As I recall, my two sisters, brother, and I broke off some ready-made switches from our fig tree for fun. We were in the back yard "spanking" the chickens when my grandfather came home and caught us in the act. These chickens were used daily to produce eggs for sale. It seemed as if he came out of nowhere. He grabbed me by the waist area and proceeded to give me a memorable lashing with his belt. Very few whippings can compare to that one. Let's just say that there are some things in life that you will never forget. That whipping was one of them.

While in a clothing store, I distinctly remember a salesman trying to win him over. The sales pitch was, "you can save $10.00 if you buy this shirt today." My grandfather's reply was, "Humph - I can save more than that if I don't buy it at all." I truly adored his passion for life and God. His instructions were always the same. If you are going to do something, do it right or don't do it at all. Nothing was more annoying to him than dealing with a phony person. He had a saying that still resonates in me today. "The emptiest wagon makes the most noise." This is evidence that many people that we encounter are living life without a mission or purpose. Hence, they are like empty wagons going nowhere.

My entire childhood was surrounded with questions about my biological father. This was a world that only existed in my brain. He lived only five miles away. He was a self-employed plumber who was never directly involved in my life. Since the first time we met, I have always called him by his first name. Although I often saw him when attending other churches with my grandfather, we never really developed a relationship. It was said that he fathered over 22 different children in the region. He was probably a great father to some of them, but not to me. I used to ride my bike over to his house seeking his attention in attempts to get to know him. We never spent more than 10 minutes together during my self-imposed visits. My mother did not want to file for child support because of all the drama that is attached to the process. She felt like it was extremely taxing on the family. She decided to rely on her faith in God and not the court system. To this day, God has never failed us as a family. He has always provided. As a result of my biological father's non-existence in my life, rejection became a staple in my adolescence. I would later learn that this was a gateway for bitterness. I grew up with a void that has taken years to comprehend.

Racism was also a constant fixture in my life since birth. I regret to say that I have experienced it frequently in my childhood and adult life. On multiple occasions, I have experienced "driving while black" as well as the case of "mistaken identity." As a result of my humble beginnings, I have learned to rely on God as the source of my resources.

By age 17, I began attending Grambling State University (Grambling, LA) ninety miles from home. I was finally free! After spending two years majoring in Music Education, I took my mother's advice and decided to switch over to Information Technology. I matriculated through the curriculum and received a Bachelors of Science degree for Computer Information Systems in 1996. During my college tenure, I led the World Famed Tiger Marching Band as a Drum Major for two consecutive years (1989-1991). I've been a member of the National Honorary Band Fraternity, Kappa Kappa Psi since 1988. I am also a former member of the U. S. Army Reserves where I served as a Tactical Computer Repairman (39Y) and Truck Driver (88M) from 1990-1995. Currently, I am a member of the International Who's Who of Professionals (2001).

College was the closest that I ever came to super stardom. As a Drum Major in the band, girls would sleep with me just because of my position. And I would let them! In my heart, I was truly a family man. But in my flesh, I was just a player! I later learned that having a bat and two balls did not guarantee that I had game. This has led to a struggle that has lasted many years, broken up good relationships, ripped apart friendships, and severed important associations. The temptation alone has proven that its strength cannot be ignored. Sometimes, a look can be as damaging as a pervasive act. Other times, words can do the damage without actions ever taking place. It has taught me a great deal about life and respect for others.

My meager beginnings have taught me to appreciate the finer things in life. I want to be everything that my father was not as it relates to fatherhood. My desire is that there is no lack in our household. God has placed me in the vanguard position to lead my family by setting a good example. I have made some mistakes that will take a lifetime to manage. In Proverbs 24:16, it reads, "For a righteous man falls seven times and rises again." It's not about how many times you fall, but rather if you decide to get back up again. It is my desire that the message in this book will inspire its readers. I am currently living through circumstances caused by my own disobedience. It is my sincere wish that the lessons learned will serve as "preventive maintenance" for others. It may be difficult to read this book and not judge the author. If I were the reader without any knowledge of the author, I would probably judge the writer because of his horrific past. Since this is not the case, I will present myself here naked and unashamed. I am a living witness that He is truly a merciful God. If He can redeem me, He can redeem anybody. This message is living evidence that God can take your mess and turn it into a miracle.

CHAPTER 2: The Spirit of Un-forgiveness

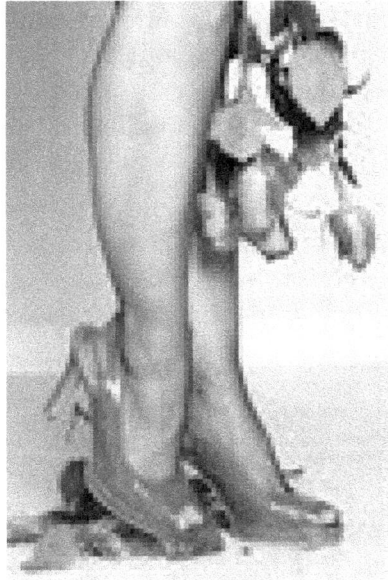

I Corinthians 6:5-7a

[5]I say this to move you to shame. Can it be that there really is not one man among you who [in action is governed by piety and integrity and] is wise and competent enough to decide [the private grievances, disputes, and quarrels] between members of the brotherhood, [6]But brother goes to law against brother, and that before [Gentile judges who are] unbelievers [without faith or trust in the Gospel of Christ]? [7]Why, the very fact of your having lawsuits with one another at all is a defect (a defeat, an evidence of positive moral loss for you). (AMP)

For months, I carried my anger around because there has been a warrant out for my arrest for a child support case. She is already getting money but constantly wants more. Since before this baby was born, we have not had a conversation outside of a superior courtroom. At this point, the thought of killing her had now become an option. I thought about it daily with no remorse. It suddenly felt right to me. If she was unwilling to allow me to move on, then why not return the favor? My heart began to fill with hatred. I wanted her to disappear and go "feed the worms." That's what dead people do. There was not a day that went by without the thought of murder. Then the spirit of the Lord stepped in! So I surrendered it all over to Him and He began to turn it around in His time…in His way…as only He can!

I have experienced the peaks and valleys of professional success. I have assisted in creating children out of wedlock and now a child through holy matrimony. I have also had my share of marriage failures, spiritual conflict, and constant battles with my faith in God. While tall, dark, and handsome to the naked eye, I even appear to be someone of affluence and stability. It might seem that way from the outside that all is well. But that is not exactly the way it is inside my heart.

The bible says in James 1:3-4 (KJV), "3Knowing this, that the trying of your faith worketh patience. 4But let patience have her perfect work, that ye may be perfect and entire, wanting nothing." Faith is not proven by how many diamonds you have. Yet, if you don't go through anything, you probably don't have anything. Faith has never been proven in abundance. A man's abundance is never measured by the accumulation of things in his life. The Lord giveth and the Lord taketh away. Faith has no way to be tried in comfort. Faith is always tested in the fiery furnace of affliction. It is proven in lack, dark days, dark hours, and tough times. You prove faith when the lights are off and the running water is cold. Your trust in God is confirmed when you have to walk to get where you're going instead of drive. In the Amplified bible, that same verse three reads, "3Be assured and understand that the trial and proving of your faith bring out endurance and steadfastness and patience." Faith will often deal with lack and how we handle it when we are forced to depend solely on God.

The kingdom suffered violence and the violent taketh by force (Matthew 11:12). This is spiritual warfare! We go to church to hear a word from God. His word helps us in driving back doubt, driving back anxiety, driving back fear, as we march by faith.

Truly, I am now like a wounded lion that must rest before embarking in another battle. However, I must now admit that the root of my pain is the spirit of un-forgiveness. Anything done with the wrong heart motive will not be effective. My senses are heightened and I have lost equilibrium. Even in this state, I am now learning how to speak the word of God all over again. In the bible, we are commanded to pray for our enemies and pray for those who persecute you. (Matthew 5:44). It is as if I have allowed God to be my last option!

In Colossians 3:13(AMP), it reads "[13]Be gentle and forbearing with one another and, if one has a difference (a grievance or complaint) against another, readily pardoning each other; even as the Lord has [freely] forgiven you, so must you also [forgive]." It is not uncommon for Christians to have questions about forgiveness. Forgiveness does not come easy for most of us. Our natural instinct is to recoil in self-protection when we've been injured. We don't naturally overflow with mercy, grace and forgiveness when we've been wronged.

Is forgiveness a conscious choice, a physical act involving the will, a feeling, or an emotional state of being? How do we forgive when we don't feel like it? How do we translate the decision to forgive into a change of heart? We forgive by faith, out of obedience. Since forgiveness goes against our nature, we must forgive by faith, whether we feel like it or not. We must trust God to do the work in us that needs to be done so that the forgiveness will be complete. Most times, however, forgiveness is a slow process. The one who suffers the most is the one who refuses to forgive. Walking in un-forgiveness is spiritual death. I believe God honors our commitment to obey Him and our desire to please him when we choose to forgive. He completes the work in his time. We must continue to forgive (our job), by faith, until the work of forgiveness (the Lord's job), is done in our hearts.

Some people walk around with un-forgiveness for years. I have heard of others taking it to their graves. Un-forgiveness is a weapon used by satan. This can lead to unnecessary arguments, legal arbitration, rumors, judgment, and even the use of private investigation into another individual's life. We can pray for God to deal with the injustices, for God to judge the person's life, and then we can leave that prayer at the altar. We no longer have to carry the anger. Although it is normal for us to feel anger toward sin and injustice, it is not our job to judge the other person in their sin. (Luke 6:37)

People that Satan couldn't get to rob a bank or shoot someone; he gets to them through strife, bitterness, resentment and un-forgiveness. These are things that many people wouldn't describe as awful sins. We look at some people and say they are a wonderful Christian, they love God, they read their Bible, they pray, and yet that person could be sinking in the quicksand of strife and un-forgiveness. Why? - Because we don't always identify it as one of the things that is a "major" sin. Yet, the scripture says that it is a device of Satan.

Paul said "forgive, lest Satan should get an advantage of us."(2 Corinthians 2:10-11). That tells us that un-forgiveness in our heart can give Satan an advantage over us, a way of controlling us, robbing us of our joy, our deliverance, our peace, our love, harmony in the home, the victory of overcoming, from possessing all of the promises of God, our prosperity, our salvation. If Satan gets an advantage, a foot hold, all of those things are stopped - all of them! At that point, what do we have to live for?
When we choose un-forgiveness, it causes us to be weighted down with debauchery. It causes one to continue to plant seeds of destruction, despair, and chaos. According to Matthew 7:1-2, what goes around always comes back around: (Matthew 7:1-2) AMP - [1]DO NOT judge and criticize and condemn others, so that you may not be judged and criticized and condemned yourselves. [2]For just as you judge and criticize and condemn others, you will be judged and criticized and condemned, and in accordance with the measure you [use to] deal out to others; it will be dealt out again to you."

Any seed planted can only produce what was originally planted. Harvest responds only to seed and not to prayer. It does not respond to fasting or to your position. Until the seed is sown, the harvest is not in view. Summer and winter exchange times. Day and night exchange positions. Cold and heat exchange seasons. Harvest time only responds to planted seeds. Psalms 89:34 declares that God will establish our seed for all generations. Yet, God will not command increase until we have committed ourselves to sowing seed. God will never bless the works of a person who continues to plant negative seeds into the lives of others. He gives to us according to the fruit of our doings (Jeremiah 17:10). It is good to plant a named financial seed for a harvest. The money seed alone will not produce a harvest. It is the word seed that determines the future of your harvest, not just the money seed. You must first plant the seed of God's word (revelation) into your heart to support any type of seed that is sown.

In my opinion, the single hardest thing to do in life is to stay in God's will; running a close second is the ability to forgive someone who has offended us. At the end of the day, we all simply want justice. We think of justice as fairness. No, No, No. Justice does not mean that a situation will be handled properly. It simply means that a payment was made for the offense. **To forgive completely, we must never hold anything against that person, ever again, or talk about it, ever bring it up again or tell anyone what they did to us.** The main reason isn't for them, but it is for us. When we don't forgive, or we don't forgive completely, then we are binding ourselves from God's blessings. We are preventing ourselves from receiving all that God has for us. Yet we parade around like someone who is in perfect standing with God. We speak in tongues and appear to be the most religious people of our era. We are like modern-day Pharisees who live out loud.

The Pharisees were often the most vocal and influential of their time. They spent their life being religious. All of us to varying degrees are religious. We have rules for which we have no scriptures. We all see God through different types of portals. We see Him through the lens of legalism, baptism, different denominations, doctrines, creeds, and concepts. Your relationship to God is directly attached to the basis of your commitment to religion. Some believe that the more you keep the law, the closer you are to God. Modern day Pharisees are religious folks. Although religious folks come from all denominations, they can be dangerous! My experience with church folks alone has proven this with resounding clarity. They can be more hateful than people you might meet in the streets that don't even know you. Listen to them talk. Some have placed themselves on a pedestal. In their minds, Heaven is only reserved for them and people who worship like them. Yet, they have committed acts in secret that they will never share out loud. Many hold grudges secretly in their hearts that they will take to their graves.

Why must we forgive? First of all, Jesus commands us to forgive. Matthew 6:14-16, says "For if you forgive men when they sin against you, your heavenly Father will also forgive you. But if you do not forgive men their sins, your Father will not forgive your sins. (NIV)" Finally, we also forgive so that our prayers will not be hindered. Forgiveness is a choice; based on obedience of God's command, that is clearly set forth in His Word... that we "walk in love". Forgiveness is the key to true spiritual freedom.

We must be free in order to enter the process of Sanctification. This process is where the believer is separated from sin and becomes dedicated to God's righteousness. We have to be free from the guilt of sin and condemnation of its activities. It is ONLY with God's grace by which the believer can do this. I don't believe that it can be 100% achieved while on the earth. It is a process that begins when we are saved and confess Jesus as our Lord and Savior. Grace is the unmerited favor in our lives. Not because we earned it, but because He thought enough of us to grant it. The result of sanctification is holiness. This is purification from guilt and the power of sin. These are the results of going after God. What does it mean to be holy? Holiness is the act of being in one mind with God! It is oftentimes referred to as spiritual training. It has more to do with the way you think as opposed to the way you look. Whatever God says is right; you agree and say its right. Whatever God says is wrong; you agree and say it's wrong. Our thoughts and ways are not His, but He gives us His word (Isaiah 55:11). So through His words, we can get His thoughts. And through His words, we can get His ways. Therefore, the word of God is the instrument by which we use to achieve holiness.

The word contains His mind. All scripture was inspired by Him. (2 Timothy 3:16) He has expressed Himself through His word. The original Greek says that every scripture is God breathed. That means the entire Bible is God breathed. Not just parts of it that you like, or don't mind applying to your life. Every single scripture is God breathed; even the part that may not agree with your particular church denomination. It is from the mouth of God. And in your hands is the very power of God that can build you up, heal your body, save your spirit, and renew your mind. In your hands is the power of God that you can put in your mouth to create your world. It can be a world that is in line with the Word of God, It can be a world that is filled with victory.

CHAPTER 3: The By-products of Bitterness

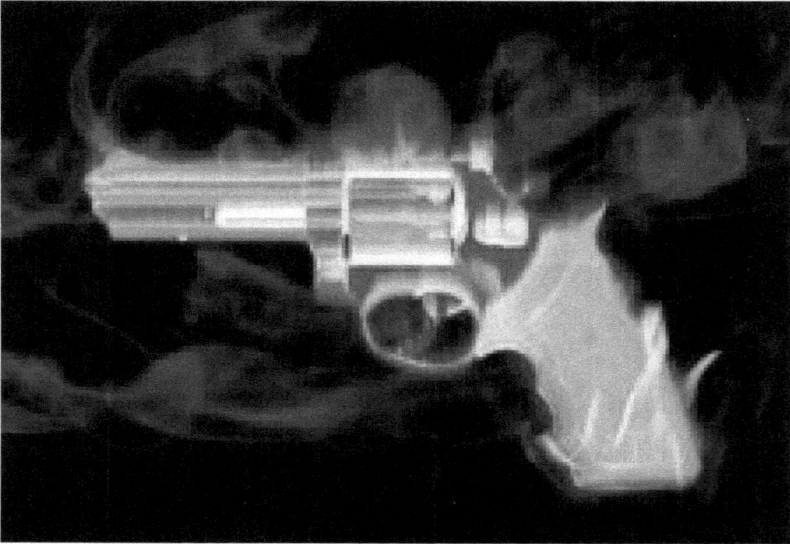

Hebrews 5:8

[8]Although He was a Son, He learned [active, special] obedience through what He suffered. (AMP)

Active anger is now considered a by-product of bitterness. A by-product is a secondary or incidental product deriving from a manufacturing process, a chemical reaction or a biochemical pathway, and is not the primary product or service being produced. A by-product can be useful and marketable, or it can have negative ecological impact.

First of all, anger is not always sin. God is angry (Psalm 7:11; Mark 3:5), and believers are commanded to be angry (Ephesians 4:26). Two Greek words are used in the New Testament for our English word "anger." One (orge) means "passion, energy;" the other (thumos) means "agitated, boiling." Webster defines anger as "excessive emotion, passion aroused by a sense of injury or wrong;" this injury may be to us or to someone else. Biblically, anger is God-given energy intended to help us solve problems. Examples of biblical anger include Paul confronting Peter because of his wrong example in Galatians 2:11-14, David being upset over hearing Nathan the prophet sharing an injustice (2 Samuel 12), and Jesus getting angry over how some of the Jews had defiled worship at God's temple in Jerusalem (John 2:13-18). Notice that none of these examples of anger involved self-defense, but defense of others or of a principle.

In the 1st chapter of Esther (AMP), King Ahasuerus was angry because his beloved queen refused to obey his command. He only wanted everyone to gaze upon her beauty for she was fair to behold. As a result of the anger that burned within, he divorced and replaced her. Anger is often a response to the perception of threat due to a physical conflict, injustice, negligence, humiliation, or betrayal. Anger may be expressed actively or passively. In the case of "active" emotion, the angry person "lashes out" verbally or physically at a target.

Just like King Ahasuerus, the mother of my first daughter is full of anger. This woman's anger burned with a fierce intensity. She used private investigators to monitor my actions twenty-four hours a day for 18 months! She began to contact anyone who was connected with me in any way including my friends, former friends, my mother and sister, business associates, and even police officials in various states based on where I was working. All of a sudden, she was more determined to contact all of my business associates and continue her barrage of lies about me while pretending to be my wife. Although we were never married, she explained to everyone that I had left my wife and unborn baby and moved to a different state. It was now apparent that if she could not receive a big payoff that her evil intentions were now to prevent me from making anymore money. Wait a minute! Doesn't every man have the right to eat? This was meant to be the coups de grace or final death blow against me in this case. Rather than it being the decisive finishing blow, it was merely another attempt at crucifying my character. When gold diggers attack, they will gamble, cheat, or even lie based on their level of frustration. It is here that they begin to shoot aimlessly at intangible targets. This is the point where she has come face-to-face with intellectual insanity. Why intellectual insanity? Regular insanity is attempting the same old thing and expecting different results. In this case, she tries a different angle every time, yet she is only traveling in circles. However, I must give her credit for one thing. She keeps coming! This is the fight of my life! In battle, odds are made by winners and losers live by them. Shhhh! I think she forgot that I am also a child of the Most High God.

She prepared her case before the baby was ever born. By the time the child was two months old, she had launched a family court child support case against me that would lead others to believe that I was a millionaire. She even hired the assistance of an attorney and private investigators to take pictures of me. Her actions displayed her concern to protect her investment ---- monthly child support checks. The information from her letters of harassment to me proves that someone is definitely monitoring my activities as I worked in Texas, Washington, DC, Pennsylvania, and New Jersey. Therefore, it was futile to attempt any communication with her without the assistance of the court.

I was already sending her $300.00 per month. She had the audacity to call me on the phone and say, "What am I supposed to do with $300?" This conversation, like almost every other one, only lasted about five minutes. My thought process was that it could be used in concert with the same amount from you (for a total of $600), baby formula, clothes, diapers, wet wipes, and medicine if needed. I added this child to my insurance only to have it refused by the mother. I attempted to send her a medical card only to have it verbally refused. This was truly an unhealthy level of hate to have in your heart. She wouldn't give a crippled crab a crutch if one of his legs were broken.☺ Since then, we have not even talked. It is now 2018.

By now, this woman has harassed me, my now ex-wife, committed prank calls to my ex-wife's job, my sister, my bank, and every place of employment, tricked my mother, and beleaguered my business partners who refused to give me any more work "because she told my business partners that she was my wife and I left her and a child." She was never my wife! Yet she has caused me to miss opportunities to put food on my family's table. She is standing behind the law and thinks that she is doing what is right. She lay down and opened up her legs for sex repeatedly without a judge and jury. But now she is responding as if she has been brutally raped and physically abused. This woman stalked me and my family since 2005 and does not appear that she will ever stop. The risk of not living in peace is that the child will find a way to blame themselves for the conflict. This is a natural reaction of a child who does not understand. I speak from the experience of blaming myself for some of my mother's problems. During my teenage years, I internalized my mother's problems as my own. I often felt that I was a part of any problem that was left unresolved. It caused me to become silent and withdrawn. Many men today are non-existent in their children's lives. This silence can be deadly. Children are naturally nurtured by their mothers; but, they are also validated by their fathers.

As a maturing Christian who understands the power of forgiveness, I wrote her a letter of forgiveness. It helped me to be released from the astigmatism that I felt for her. She used that letter to get an order of protection against me. Orders of Protection are another trick by custodial parents to delay or prevent visitation through the court system. She protected herself and contact information from me, which means that I cannot contact her or the child without being arrested. Of course, through modern technology, I am always able to get any information that I need.

At any rate, my feelings of resentment were becoming more intense with each passing moment. I immediately wrote a response to show my disgust to the court system hoping that it would get the judge's attention. It did not work. For months, I carried my anger around because there has been a warrant out for my arrest due to a contempt of court charge. At this point, the thought of murder had now become an option. I thought about it daily. It suddenly felt right to me. If she was unwilling to allow me to move on, then why not return the favor? My heart began to fill with hatred for this person. I wanted her to disappear. I even choreographed a plan. I soon destroyed it because my conscious (Holy Spirit) overpowered that plan. Thank God for divine intervention!

Hell hath no fury like a woman scorned! While many attribute this quote to William Shakespeare, it actually comes from a play called the "The Mourning Bride" (1697) by William Congreve. The complete quote is "Heaven has no rage like love to hatred turned, nor hell a fury like a woman scorned." I would like to paraphrase a concept used by R & B singer R. Kelly in one of his songs, "One mad woman can make another woman hate ALL men."

As if that was not enough, I also started experiencing conflict on my job. The I.T. organization that provided employment for me all of a sudden did not need me anymore. Isn't it ironic that I was the only black face on the payroll of over 130 people? Upon my resignation, they immediately cut off my insurance plan. Now that made me angry. I even filed a racial discrimination lawsuit against them that did not end well for me. (go figure)

Anger breeds condescension which evolves into bitterness. Once bitterness is conceived, the heart fills with hatred towards the target. Hate is never expressed through words…only action. Where does bitterness come from? Bitterness comes when the adversity that is on the outside has now gotten on the inside. Now the inner man is contaminated by the experiences that you went through on the outside. You can't keep it out of you. You began to sink into something that you should have passed through. It is now in you. It is called a root of Bitterness. In Hebrews 12:14-15, it reads, [14]Follow peace with all men, and holiness, without which no man shall see the Lord: [15]Looking diligently lest any man fail of the grace of God; lest any root of bitterness springing up trouble you, and thereby many be defiled(KJV). Verse 15 challenges us to look diligently into our own heart to check for bitterness. Our attitude about people affects our ability too see God. As long we have discord with people, the less we are able see God. The confusion affects your ability to see the Lord. Bitterness is a cycle that short circuits our connection with God. How can bitterness be destroyed? Bitterness can ONLY be destroyed by replacing it with the Fruit of the Spirit. The fruit will destroy the root. Long-suffering destroys the root of bitterness. Long-suffering is easier said than done. For it is the ability to deal respectively with others over prolonged periods of time. While in Texas, I remember my first work opportunity. I was working remotely for a guy who lived in Houston but serviced a client in Seattle, Washington. I only agreed to work with him because I was waiting for other I.T. jobs to surface. Since we had not signed a contractual agreement, he decided not to pay me. I sent a formal notice of my intent to sue and he then changed his mind. Although I finally received payment for my efforts, this could have all been avoided with a simple contract. (Amos 3:3). It requires a coordinated effort between two or more like-minded individuals.

I have had a history of success in Dallas, Texas. I was a member of The Potter's House under Bishop T. D. Jakes. I joined the recording choir and we performed with excellence. We even completed a musical cd project called, "On A Wing and A Prayer." I also met a wonderful man affectionately known as "Captain." He helped me get into the seafood business. Though my earnings were slow, it gave me hope like never before. He gave me optimism at my very lowest point of that season in my life. Like car tires, my thoughts needed realignment. In order for my situation to change, I have to begin thinking different thoughts. For the last 18 years, my thinking has never been consistently good. It has been good, bad, focused, reckless, tamed, wild, and sometimes stagnant. In order for my breakthrough to come, my thinking has to be renewed. According to 2 Corinthians 10:4 - [4]For the weapons of our warfare are not physical [weapons of flesh and blood], but they are mighty before God for the overthrow and destruction of strongholds. [5]Casting down imaginations, and every high thing that exalteth itself against the knowledge of God, and bringing into captivity every thought to the obedience of Christ; (AMP).

Imaginations are actually images. The image on the inside feeds our thinking. The only way to overcome bad images is to replace them with positive words. Bad thoughts only get replaced with bad thoughts unless we speak positively to them. These images can be used to keep us from transforming our minds into new thinking. Thoughts are habit-forming processes that are seen through human expression. In other words, how we act determines what we are thinking on the inside.

I believe that every man and woman has the ability to change. Yet, it seems that we find it hard to commit to this new way. Although our brain focuses on whatever we feed it, there is a constant battle with the fleshly nature in which we were born. It takes the grace of God upon our lives to overcome the flesh. My problems were born out of this internal struggle.

My life has really changed over the last few years. I went from believing that I was all that and a bag of chips to seeing that I wasn't even a chip in the bag. I was feeling lost and cold to the human touch. It is a point where there is no desire to interact with others in a meaningful way. It is likened unto the state of a zombie or a robot who cannot think freely. And way back in the recesses of my mind hidden from the rest of society I was thinking," where are you God? Where is the God that saved my family, friends, co-workers, and others from unfavorable circumstances? Where art thou? Does not thou hearest me? No……………really! For real! Where the hell are you? Don't you see me down here drifting into nothingness?" Then, I became bold enough to say it out loud in the privacy of my own home. Sometimes while driving down the highway I would murmur or even scream depending on what time of the day it was. My mind raced for miles to get to nowhere all day long. I eventually decided that I no longer wanted to be here and planned suicide. I calmly typed a suicide note on my computer. After printing it off, I sat in the back yard on a tree stump with my gun in hand. I was actually ready to assassinate myself.

I waited silently to hear a Rhema word from God. It didn't come and I did not want to go out like this. Contract work had been severely scarce for me. For the entire year, I only worked about 5 ½ months. We were making it on my ex-wife's unemployment checks and hope in God. I repeated this process daily several times over. I even shot into the air on some days to verify that the gun was fully operational. My ex-wife and I argued constantly about this and other topics. It seemed more difficult to get through each day. My mood swings were far worse than a woman pregnant in her 3rd trimester waiting for her water to break. It seemed that my water was blocked by the Hoover Dam. I was a combustible nightmare waiting to happen. I awakened each morning ready to explode. I could actually hear explosions in my sleep. My mind was warped. I could not focus on work, my marriage, or anything of importance without being thoroughly distracted. I even remember going out to buy beer, a condom, and paying for a call girl to give me pleasure. It was just easier than arguing, making up, and eventually getting around to love-making with my ex-wife.

Throughout this whole process, I have allowed my anger to spin me out of control. My focus was on the problems of my past, concern for my future, and the pain of my present. I have yielded to the bitterness that has been down on the inside. I have allowed it to infect me and my household. I have internalized every part of this. It has caused devastation to my life, my beautiful family, beliefs as a Christian, and my marriage covenant relationship with God. The root of my problem has been a result of not trusting in God 100%. Until now, I have only given God about 80% of me during fleeting moments of obedience. Obedience gives birth to blessings. The blessings represent the anointing and empowerment from God. Although I was never perfectly consistent, it was never obvious to the naked eye before now. In only the 3rd year of marriage, my ex-wife and I were torn apart because of the root of bitterness. My ex-wife selfishly vexed me into moving to a city where she could address all of her issues without a thought of any of mine. Somewhere along the way, she convinced herself that she did a good thing. SO NOW….When your ex-wife gives all of herself, she believes that you do not have a right to disrespect the marriage. When you do, it causes her to reveal the secrets of her personality that have never before been revealed…maybe not even to her. My ex-wife left 2 weeks after my family's reunion and took every dime I had accumulated. She also closed out the corporate bank accounts and redirected my current paychecks. How? She was able to do this because I had trusted her as a business partner. Trust is a small word with a big meaning. Previously, she exclaimed over and over the last few years that we had been together that, "I would never do like the other women you have dealt with. I am not interested in what I can get from you." Lie, lie, and lie! It's okay that we broke up, but it is now evident that she was attempting to choke the financial life out of me. She took our baby and my hard earned wages. She amassed some $19,995 from my work. With an ex-wife like this, who needs enemies? Furthermore, she had the nerve to call it legal. But, we all know that old saying, what goes around always come back around (derived from Matthew 7:1-2).

People don't always mean what they say. Very rarely do some ever say what they really feel. Not knowing certain things can create interruptions in the communication process. Interruptions are formal challenges that can influence relationships. This occurs either by strengthening the bond or breaking it into pieces. The major problem in life is learning how to handle the costly interruptions. The door that slams shut, the marriage that failed, or the plan that got sidetracked. What about that lovely poem that did not get written because someone knocked on your door?

God always puts a challenge in place to stretch our trust in him. Trust is also a complicated word. It involves the risk of relinquishing control that we are accustomed to having at our fingertips. When He wants us to trust Him, He allows circumstances to happen in our lives that force us to re-prioritize. It is only a test that we're going through. How we handle each test determines how much more He will place in our care.

My newborn baby daughter is away from me now. I feel as though I am assisting in creating an angel without wings. I am least upset about the failed marriage, but most disheartened by the relationship that "would have been" established through this child. Although children tend to cling to their mothers, they can only truly be defined by their fathers. It is the father's DNA and blood type that resides in the child. Otherwise, there would be no need for a paternity test to prove that he is the father.

My ex-wife hit me really hard through this ordeal. It has affected my finances, spiritual walk, emotions, confidence, self-esteem, and physical presence. Mentally I was in crisis, out of crisis, and back in crisis again! I lost all traces of normality and standardized thinking. I absolutely lost mental consciousness for several days. I was almost at the point of giving up on God, but refused to say it out loud.

It caused me to step outside of myself and evaluate who I have become. As I reviewed the evidence of my actions, I looked like a fool! The stupidity of my efforts far outweighs the literal concept of sanity. This has been a vicious cycle of madness. If it were an entrée in a restaurant, it would be a full plate of self-destruction with a side of ridiculousness. It is quite embarrassing to talk about it openly. However, I am only doing this out of obedience to God. But I was taught that God doesn't make mistakes. And sometimes, out of His tender mercy, He uses our painful experiences to reveal more of Himself to us. It is my desire that my stupidity will be transformed into revelation for someone else. My character must be reshaped in order for me to reach my destiny. You'll never rise above the limitations of your character. Your character will determine your anointing, your prosperity, and your destiny. God will never bless you above where your character can sustain you.

I now realize that I have been having an "outer court" experience with Our Father. I have not pierced the veil of my flesh. Christians must choose whether to have an outer court, inner court, or Holy of Holies (behind the veil) experience with God. The presence of God must be practiced at home in addition to weekly worship services. People who have an outer court relationship with God will not experience breakthrough. It is because we either don't spend time with Him or we stopped spending time with Him. I have to press into the anointing of God for my life so that I may be obedient to His voice. This can only come as I am faithful with God's written word. The pre-requisite to ever hearing a Rhema (spoken) word from God is faithfulness with His written word. God's word is our escort into the intimate place to get a word from Him. Remember: Breakthrough comes when God's word begins to speak to our situation!

Roy Jones is one of my favorite boxers. His description of a true champion is one who can come back from the worst loss ever as if nothing ever happened. It is either champion or loser for me now. I refuse to be defeated. I will not wallow in confusion. God is not the author of confusion. Just me, myself, and I right now. Alas, Master, How shall we do? (2 Kings 6:15-16). When Elisha's servant Elijah looked out from among their camp, he only saw men on horses and chariots. But the prophet Elisha saw the men surrounded by God's Army of Angels. I have to use my angels now in spiritual warfare to deal with my trouble.

Trouble is a burden that the anointing removes. In times of trouble we must run and hide in the presence of God. When we do, He will hide us in the secret of His setting, in the secret of His tent, in the secret of His dwelling place. And while we are there, He will keep us safe. In David's time God lived in buildings made by men's hands. But change was on the horizon. Because of the death, burial and resurrection of Jesus, God no longer dwells in places made by men's hands. The Anointed One, Jesus, has made it so that God now dwells in us. 2 Corinthians 6:16 says, "... for ye are the temple of the living God; as God hath said, I will dwell in them, and walk in them; and I will be their God, and they shall be my people." (KJV) His anointing lives in me!

It is the anointing that saved Jesus. After He quoted Isaiah 61:1, and said these things are fulfilled in your ears, the people grabbed Him and tried to throw Him off a cliff. But they found they couldn't do it. The Bible said He walked right through them. Now all the time they were trying to grab Him, something kept them from touching Him.

I want to get to a place where I hear His voice and immediately obey. His words have to become a lamp unto my feet for every step that I take. This guidance will then be a light unto the path of my future. God's secrets are not available for everybody. He intends for every person to be able to have access to it, but you have to have a key to open the door to it. And that key is being in right standing with Him.

I don't know where I will be years from now. I just hope that it's in Him!

CHAPTER 4: The Power of Words

Hebrews 11:3

³By faith we understand that the worlds [during the successive ages] were framed (fashioned, put in order, and equipped for their intended purpose) by the word of God, so that what we see was not made out of things which are visible. (AMP)

One of many President Barack Obama's quotes is, "A good compromise, a good piece of legislation, is like a good sentence; or a good piece of music. Everybody can recognize it." Although actions speak louder than words, it does not negate the effective power of the spoken word. Words are life or death. The power of life and death are in the tongue. Once words are released, then they are no longer in our possession. They become community property. The same way that words were used by God to frame the world in which we live is the same way that words work for us. If you speak negatively, you will have a life of darkness. (Matthew 15:18) If you are a positive speaking person, then you will be looked upon as a source of light and strength. People will always want to be around you.

Words are a catalyst that causes a multitude of events to occur. In Luke 17:1, it reads "[1]Then said he unto the disciples, it is impossible but that offences will come: but woe unto him, through whom they come! (KJV)" In other words, temptations, snares, traps set to entice to sin are sure to come. Yet, the word illustrates here that affliction is the reward for those who are the offenders of the brethren.

In every conflict, someone has to be the Lamb. There must be a sacrifice in order for Atonement to begin. Even when we feel justified, we can never strike out against another soul without wounding ourselves. We must remember that all things in existence have a specific protocol. These protocols act as boundaries that dictate the various activities that may take place within a particular season or location. For instance, reformation or the act of being reformed takes place inside of rooms dedicated to confinement. Atonement generally occurs once per year during a specific season. In the physical world, we usually think of four dimensions: length, width, height, and time. In the life God has in mind for us, love is our primary weapon. It is the assured defense against any offense. God wants us to dwell in the love zone. Love fueled by understanding leads to peace and tranquility. Think of Christmas time when everyone at least attempts to be kind to one another simply based on the season of the year. We must take account of every careless word uttered while here on earth (Matthew 12:35-45). Be careful what you say in the "heat of the moment."

In the court of law, words either become the weapon or can be used as a foundation for defense. Either way, they play an important role. One wrong word can send you to jail. One right word can break a case wide open. The right set of words can even cause you to get a new trial when things are not going your way. Sometimes you can speak the right words, but be the wrong messenger. I found this out the hard way. For three long years, my attempts to represent myself in court proved to be lethal. I finally found a lawyer to represent me. The only reason I chose this lawyer is because when I reviewed her website, she appeared to be a free thinker. She was practicing criminal as well as family law. This is just what the doctor ordered. In the event that I went cuckoo for cocoa puffs, she could also represent me in a murder trial (LOL). Well, at least I wouldn't have to worry about getting the electric chair. Since I started writing this book in 2008, it appears that only thirty-one states that use it. Hopefully that statement will always remain a running joke without the possibility of ever becoming a reality. At any rate, she wrote several books. This meant that she was an open minded person. Therefore, I chose her based on those credentials.

My freedom was now being threatened. I feel compelled to move quickly with maximum precision. Up under the weight of the cross, Jesus spoke the words "Tel-telesti," which means "It is finished." These were Jesus' final words. I felt like it was over for my life. I awaken each morning with the spirits of evil taunting me. Then I pray and cast out demons that represent the spirit of murder. I also speak positive affirmations over my family's livelihood so that we can have a normal day. Yeah right! I don't even know what normal is anymore. Normal for me is now some kind of fight, resistive confrontation, argument with someone somewhere about something that I probably don't even care about, and dealing with just plain ignorant people. But, the word of God says to deal in love with your brothers and sisters. Through it all, I still smile because no-one can steal the joy that comes from the Lord. A smile on my face does not mean that the hurt has been erased. I now know what it means when people say, "Somebody's got to be the Lamb of sacrifice."

I never knew that life could be this difficult. If I had my choice, I would have asked to be somebody's pet. Some pets get better treatment than humans. They get to ride in the front seat of their master's car. They get their own cage or house where meals are served daily. They take pictures and go on family vacations. They have their own tailor-made outfits. Everybody competes to show them affection. They generally don't get whippings and have shorter life spans. They don't have to go to work everyday. Get this....some of them even have animal insurance! Isn't that amazing? They go to the Veterinarian on a regular basis. Some of us do not even have steady medical and dental insurance. When they die, there is a funeral, a death certificate, and a time of mourning. What a way to go!

God often works behind the scenes in hard times to prepare you, train you, teach you patience, and develop your character. When you learn how to hang on through the difficult times, you'll get to see His goodness. This is a difficult pill to swallow because we are sometimes looking for immediate gratification. Yet, He generally makes us wait for the solution prescribed through His will.

If you have wondered what the real problem is for me, I will tell you now. I have always believed that the truth of God's word will deliver me from all things. I was dead wrong! The word plants an image on the inside. The problem is that I stopped meditating on the word. This is mainly due to "giving up" on the image inside because it tries your patience and causes doubt to enter the mind. Worry is the opposite of patience. It evens fosters negative meditation. I used to have an image on the inside of a better life. But it has been tainted by my struggle. Each week I go to church and hear the word. Satan comes immediately to steal out the Word that was sown in my heart. (Mark 4:15). This verse of scripture was written only to those who hear the word and no one else. He does not address anyone who doesn't receive or hear the word. The image must be cultivated by not allowing doubt to enter the mind. The 2nd thought (doubt) comes from reasoning. Don't reason with yourself! The more you meditate on the word of God, the more success you have. The inward person must be protected. Living a prosperous life involves the word. The word is going to give you knowledge. The knowledge is going to give you expectation or hope. Once you get the hope, then faith has something to feel. Breakthrough doesn't come just because we know the truth. Breakthrough comes when God's word begins to speak to our situation! Christians will always have to face the truth test. Ye shall know the truth and the truth shall set you free (John 8:32). Just knowing the truth will not set you free. If you continue in the word, then you'll be made free. Freedom does not come because you know the truth. Freedom comes because you continue in the truth. Total breakthrough won't come until you keep on doing it. Here we want more than mere penetration. We require total breakthrough. You just have to keep on doing it over and over and over again!

I now recognize that this is just another trick of the enemy trying to steal my praise. My present enemies are working overtime to harm me. In the spiritual realm, this is one big farceur. That's right…one big joke. The satanic forces that exist use situations to draw us out from the hedge of protection that God has given to us. It is only then that he is able to cause chaos in our lives. Yet, we render him powerless, as he truly is, when we remain steadfast on the word of God. This is easier said than done. One simple test is when we get mad at others. It is here that satan can cause us to become ineffective. We will never mature to the place God intended for our lives until we learn the art of forgiveness.

Forgiveness is the divine miracle of grace. Resentment, that is, un-forgiveness is a silent destroyer of many Christian's lives. Understanding God's forgiveness to you through Christ is critical when attempting to forgive others. How can you just forgive someone for committing an offense without retaliation? To the natural mind that seems impossible. Doesn't the Bible teach an eye for an eye? We are also taught in church that God won't forgive us if we don't forgive those who wronged us. This is a startling dilemma! Why is it so hard to forgive? As soon as I see THAT person or THAT thing, my emotions become active with animosity, resentment, and pain. It is not wise to spread your resentment for one person to others. You may be inclined to resent those who are associated with the person you are trying to forgive. This feeling does not give you the right to mistreat their family or friends when we see them.

The process of forgiveness involves four key elements. They are recognition, repentance, restitution, and reconciliation. First, there must be recognition of sin. When we recognize our own sin, we *must* also recognize God's corresponding grace to us. Next is <u>repentance</u>, that is, a measurable change in behavior. Depending upon the nature of the offense that may lead to <u>restitution</u>, which is a biblical principle. In the Old Testament, if someone stole one sheep, he had to give back four. Although this is not always possible, it is the right thing to do. The ultimate goal of all of the above is <u>reconciliation</u>.

There is truly an art to forgiveness. Forgiveness is conditioned on repentance and the willingness to make reparations, or atonement. The effect of forgiveness is the restoration of both parties to the former state of relationship. The Hebrew word for forgive means to pardon or spare. The Greek word for forgive means to send forth, lay aside, let go, or omit. (Proverbs 25:21-22 NIV), "[21]If your enemy is hungry, give him food to eat; if he is thirsty, give him water to drink. [22]In doing this, you will heap burning coals on his head, and the LORD will reward you." The phrase "Heap burning coals on his head" was a horrible punishment reserved for the wicked (Psalm 140:10). Here, however, it is kindness that will hurt the enemy, that is, the reciprocation of good for evil that will win him over (cause him to repent).

We are comprised of what is called a triune being. We are a spirit with a soul that lives in a body. Our soul is made of (1) Mind, (2) Will, and (3) Emotions. We are spiritual beings having a human experience. God gave us a free will because He commanded us to have dominion over the earth. How can we do this except that He can trust us to operate as mature beings in the earth? Everyday will bring new challenges, opportunities, or both. They are all under our control. A soft answer turns away wrath. Sometimes it is not what you say, but how you say it. Time is our most precious commodity. Once it is gone, you will never get it back. Likewise, words are our greatest asset. Their value cannot be measured. They are mathematical in nature. Words have the power to divide, multiply, add, or subtract from its target. Use them wisely!

CHAPTER 5: The costs of Change

Genesis 32: 24, 30

24And Jacob was left alone, and a Man wrestled with him until daybreak. 30And Jacob called the name of the place Peniel, [the face of God], saying, For I have seen God face to face, and my life is spared *and* not snatched away. (AMP)

One day I was driving home from work at a client's site in Charleston, SC. I overheard a legion of devils speaking. They asked, "Will God help him?" No matter what anyone believes, I heard them as clear as a bell. At that moment, I became utterly discouraged. This was a moment of clarity. I now knew that the only way to truly enjoy life was to start making some changes. Otherwise, how would God get any glory out of this? Interstate 26 will never again be the same for me. It was a tantalizing moment where I felt broken. I now know what it feels like to be delivered but damaged.

A conversation with my mother a few weeks later has created a new-found conviction in me. My mother found out the details of my woman problems and current negative behavior. My mother called to speak with me. Under the calmness of her voice, I detected an unpleasant undertone. She gave me some shocking news about my biological father's death in 1995. Her words were like a silent alarm deep down in the recesses of my spirit. She had never spoken to me like that in all of my years. Since the call happened yesterday, it was still fresh in my mind. She said in a very stern 65 year old voice, "I never thought that I would have to consider burying any of my children in connection with AIDS or anything like that. But what you are doing is not in God's plan. You can't walk around calling yourself a minister and act like that. There are strangers out there who only want your money and anything else they can get out of you. I never felt a need to tell you why Sam died of a heart attack. But now I do. He was taking some kind of sexual enhancement pills and sleeping around on his 2nd wife. When he died, he was in the bed with another woman whom he had been messing around with for the last several years. It was really ugly and not something to share with everybody. I just wanted you to know that's who he was. But you have got to live up to your calling. You get yourself together and get home to be with your family. That's the end of the sermon for tonight! I'll talk to you later. Good-bye!" She then proceeded to hang up the phone. I sat there in shock as the cold chills palpitated through my lifeless body. I made an appointment to get help with "internal anger issues." So for the first time in my life, I went to see a professional licensed therapist.

One of many President Barack Obama's quotes is, "Change will not come if we wait for some other person or some other time. We are the ones we've been waiting for. We are the change that we seek." In May of 2007, I went to visit with Pastor Mike Rozell of

40

† He spent 1 ½ hours casting demons out of me and teaching me how to do it on my own. I was instantly delivered from ghastly demons that were stunting my growth in the word of God. I was happy for about 24 hours. However they returned and I had to repeat this process weekly, then daily, then almost by the hour. Finally I realized that renewing my mind daily will sometimes consist of casting out demons.

There is a saying in Christian Dom that goes "New levels bring about new devils." I have grown exponentially since I began writing this book a year ago. Everything and everyone has the ability to grow. If you recall the book of Genesis, satan took the form of a serpent. But even he was allowed to grow and mature into something more over time. In the 12th chapter of Revelation, he grew up to become a dragon. During a war with the archangels, he was kicked out of heaven. Yet, he was still powerful enough to take 1/3 of heaven's angels along with him with one swipe of his tail. Now let's let a closer look at this number. In the 5th chapter of Revelation, God has created for Himself 10,000 times 10,000 and thousands of thousands of angels. That's 100,000,000 (100 million) by thousands of thousands which can be identified as an infinite number. So, it is obvious by this calculation that 1/3 of this infinite number is pretty large....at least several hundred millions. No wonder it is possible for defeated devils to return with 7 additional spirits even more powerful than themselves (Matthew 12:43-45).

I have to constantly cast devils out of my soul (mind, will, and emotions). Thoughts of hate and murder haunt me daily. I awaken each morning and cast out these devils (demons) by speaking to them in a forceful tone of voice. If you have demons, simply call them by name and rebuke them in the name of Jesus. "Spirit of murder, I rebuke you now in the Mighty name of Jesus, Come out of me now!" You sometimes have to repeat this over and over again. Demons get in through our physical openings. This includes eyes, ears, nose, and mouth. When reprimanded, they have to leave through the same openings that allowed them entrance. When they are forced to go, they will depart as liquid forms (saliva or as tears), screams (loud noises), and yawning (because they have to be breathed out of your system).

Although this probably reminds you of an excerpt from the "The Exorcist" movie, it is totally accurate. This is because many times demons enter our minds without our knowledge. This is truly spiritual warfare. The battlefield is in my mind. This is a really difficult situation. The most embarrassing part of this is that I am filled with the word of God. Yet, I seem to get angry every time I think about personal problems. When I minister in the local prisons, I persistently remind them that I am only one bad decision away from sitting in a cell next to them. This is why it is important that I renew my mind daily.

Even when we feel justified, it is not good to trade evil for evil. It always has a nocuous effect on any situation. It only serves to cause intense harm to its victims. In Galatians 6:10, it reads, "¹⁰So then, as occasion and opportunity open up to us, let us do good [morally] to all people [not only being useful or profitable to them, but also doing what is for their spiritual good and advantage]. Be mindful to be a blessing, especially to those of the household of faith [those who belong to God's family with you, the believers] (AMP)." It is impossible to lash out negatively against someone else without wounding yourself. You see, an evil man cannot speak good things because there is not any good in his heart. In Matthew 12:35-36, it says that "³⁵ the good man out of his good treasure brings forth good, and the evil man out of his evil treasure brings forth evil. ³⁶ I tell you, on the Day of Judgment men will render account for every careless word they utter (KJV)." Therefore, whatever we have spoken must be accounted for when we stand before God at the Throne of Grace.

The wrong words can speak death to our own souls. It is the feeling of being forsaken. This feeling is a part of the process. Anybody can walk with God when His presence is manifest. The real challenge is to walk with Him when His presence is not manifest.

You need faith when you don't see Him, can't feel Him, when you have run out of unemployment, when you can't find employment, when your children are acting up, when they are about to take the house, the car, and the dog.

Up under the weight of his attack, even Jesus cried out, "Eli, Eli, Lamasabathany" – Translated this means My God, My God, Why has thy forsaken me? This is Jesus, the water-walker, the leper cleanser, the healer, the miracle worker. However, He was at his lowest point right here during the time when he was to give his life for our salvation. This is the only time in the bible that Jesus referred to God as God. Every other time, he called Him Father or some other title. But, here in the midst of this moment, he cried out to the heavens for help. When real pressure comes into your life, the true character comes out. Every situation will either make you bitter or better. We all have a private region in our life that we shield from everyone else. It is here that we must come face to face with the apparent reality of who we are. It is here that we have to be naked and unashamed about our individual nature.

I would previously shrink from the battle under the weight of pressure. But now, after countless mistakes, I have been forced to come to grips with the reality of my life. The bible says that we are more than conquerors (Romans 8:37). That means that we have to overcome our situations by conquering them. When an opponent is defeated, he does not go away. He is simply stopped for a season. Therefore, the struggle continues until he is conquered. Demons exist and are real. They are disembodied spirits that require a body to take action. Standing on the word of God against demonic forces causes them to flee from us. The only way to deal with pressure is to stand on the word of God. But it requires patience to get to the other side. I can directly relate 99% of my problems in my life to impatience. The highest form of discipline is learning to wait on God.

God started a good work in me several years ago. I started this other mess through disobedience to God's word. However, He is merciful. He is Alpha and Omega. He is the Beginning and the End. He is the Author and Finisher of my faith. He that began a good work in me shall perform it until the day of Jesus Christ. I am not in this by myself! I am casting all of my cares upon Him. This gives me hope.

Hope is a dream. Have you ever had a pleasant dream? You may have dreamed of walking out of a bad situation, or living totally pain free. Or perhaps you dream of being totally debt free, or owning your own business. Tangible hope is having confident expectation. You will always have circumstances in which the enemy will try to embezzle your joy. Your reaction to that is to rejoice in hope. Hope is the fuel that feeds your faith. The Word says in Hebrews 11:1, "Now faith is the substance of things hoped for..." Faith gives substance to hope and forces it to become a reality.

You get hope from the word of God. The word of God is the only source I know that always gives you hope. When you turn on the television news, it doesn't always give you hope. But if that is your only source of information you can end up hopeless. The word of God, however, always gives you hope. Every time you open your Bible you can find hope for the future.

In the bible, Jacob wrestles with an angel of God. This depicts the process of sincere faithfulness, from self-sufficiency to total surrender to God's presence. Jacob's wrestling match is a present-day version of man's struggle within. Here we witness the power of God's grace. For it was only by His grace that the darkness within Jacob's heart was dispelled. Jacob himself called on God and it became a one night standoff with an angel. After being visited, Jacob limped away. However, he limped away with a new name, Israel, which means, "he who struggled with God and has overcome." Though this parable is nothing less than spectacular, it illustrates just how determined he was. This is significant because Jacob's life was transformed. I admire his courage to do something different. He went from a trickster to a man with new beginnings.

Up until now, there has been a huge gulf between myself and Jesus. While walking the earth, He was too holy to live in sin. Throughout most of my adult life, I have been too sinful to live in holiness. We were separated by our state. He was in a perpetual state of holiness. We were like two different kinds. While I am here, let me make this point regarding interracial relationships. Love is color blind. There is nothing wrong with a brown dog loving a white dog. If they mate, the offspring may be of a different color, but it is still a dog. On the contrary, a dog should not mate with a chicken. They are of two different kinds. Animals that bark should not try to fly. When it comes to love, there is nothing wrong with interracial marriages. This is a matter of personal preference. Love is still love in any color regardless of the environment. Just make sure that it is love and not infatuation.

God gives us different levels of grace based on whether or not we have entered into covenant with Him. Today, we refer to different races as Japanese, Chinese, Anglo-Saxons, Afrikaans, Russian, Indians, Latinos, Mexicans, Caribbean, Italians, African-Americans, and too many others to name. In the Old Testament, people were referred to as Jews or Gentiles. Those that are in covenant were called Jews. Those that were out of covenant were called Gentiles (non-Jews). Because all God really cares about is whether or not you know Him. Everything else is immaterial to God. The Hebrews were the only ones distinguished by having an unseen God. Every other people worshipped a God that was visible or man-made.

According to the bible, all that is in the world is (1) Lust of the flesh, (2) Lust of the eye, and (3) The Pride of Life. These are the only categories where we can be tempted. Your highest moment is only a sign that you are about to face your greatest temptation. The problem with temptation is curiosity. The enemy tempts us with people that we later become disgusted with. You believe that the grass is greener on the other side. However, after multiple failures, you realize that it is a path that you have already experienced. The enemy comes while you are building your future. The past will antagonize you with something you thought you got away from. Most of the time when we panic God redirects us back to the power that He has already given to us. Many times we have been delayed but not denied! The setback is only a setup for a comeback. Pragmatic concepts serve as a launching pad for our life because success is intentional.

God has the power to move quickly to deliver us from evil. When we show him that we are willing to do better, He will snatch you out of your drug habit, out of the bed of some lover, or anything that has your attention. He looks at us as a peculiar treasure or unique people because we obey His voice (Exodus 19:3-6).

As it relates to holiness, I now feel coerced to live a righteous life. Not because I have arrived, but merely because there is an obligation prompted by God's grace on my life. I now understand why it is important to view my body as a tabernacle. The term tabernacle in the Hebrew is Ohel Moedh, which literally means tent of meeting. This is referred to as a place of general assembly. It is the place where humanity and divinity come together. It is a dating place where a fallen man can rendezvous with God. Sin separates us from God's presence. This is the gulf previously mentioned because I was in a state of sin. The bible talks about death on several different occasions. Yet, it is not referring to physical death. It is actually talking about a separation. Physical death only occurs when the spirit within us separates from our body. Death in the bible generally means something that was inside of something else has been pulled apart and the breech between the two has caused death. Being spiritually dead is when the human spirit has been separated from the spirit of God. At that moment, you can become spiritually dead although you are still physically alive. When we sin, it immediately disconnects us from God. It is like having a dislocated shoulder. The two parts are no longer fused together anymore. Sin was a generational curse inherited from Adam. This is why we never have to teach our children to sin. They don't need to go to school or a workshop to learn how to lie because we are born into sin and shaped in iniquity. Regardless of race, color, or creed, we are all traced back to Adam's seed. There is a potential to do evil that I have not even contemplated. It only takes the right situation or circumstance to make it manifest. Some of us have even discovered them and refuse to talk about it. We don't want to say anything that will jeopardize our faith.

What does it mean to have eternal life? It is not where I am going to spend the rest of my life. It is something that I am supposed to have right now. When I got saved on the altar, God gave me eternal life at that moment. It means that I am eternally fused back together with God. Jesus is our righteousness and we are complete in Him. The words Reconcile, Redeem, Renew, and Restore are predicated on a love story that reconnects God back to humanity. That is why they all start with the prefix "RE." The only way we are disconnected is through the 3rd party of sin.

In the past three years, I have missed more exits while driving, run more red lights, experienced daydreams and nightmares than the average person will during the natural course of their entire life. All of this was a direct result of sin that was prevalent in my life. The singular sin is a state whereas, the plural sins represent actions. Our personal blunders cause frustration in secret places. There are five different types of baggage that impact our walk with God.

I.   Baggage of Sin   - Actions that break our rest and communion with God.
II.   Baggage of Guilt   - Unwilling to be forgiven for faults.
III.   Baggage of Pride   - Self-Image, Arrogance, usually hidden from the public.
IV.   Baggage of Dreams - The weight of dreaming much bigger than my reality.
V.   Baggage of Responsibilities – Standard accountabilities of life.

Under the weight of our baggage, the fabric of our character is revealed. Love gives and lust taketh away. This is obvious when someone is emotionally detached and lustfully selfish. They often sow indifference hoping to reap affection. They plant the seed of deception desiring to gain trust. These actions alone prove that the perpetrator is spiritually lost.

The bible tells us that God is hidden from us. He cannot be explained, but must be revealed. In 2 Corinthians 4:3-4, it reads, "But if our gospel be hid, it is hid to them that are lost: In whom the gospel of this world hath blinded the minds of them which believe not, lest the light of the glorious gospel of Christ, who is the image of God, should shine unto them (KJV)." As Christians, our reality is like a lie to those that are lost. They cannot see the truth. They look at us as being abnormal. God has opened up his wisdom to us. They don't understand how we can praise a God that we cannot see. This is because the more that God is revealed, the more we change. The more we see of Him, the more we become like Him. Once you come into contact with the presence of God, no one on earth can convince you otherwise. He changes your personality, attitude, and way of thinking.

God is omnipresent and the enemy cannot hide Him from us. Therefore, the only hope that the devil has is to try to cover our eyes. He tries to blind us with issues, weaknesses, and problems to distort our vision. You cannot build your future in the dark. Anything that affects your vision is going to impair your mobility. Without a vision, the people perish for the lack of knowledge. Rationalization is the enemy of revelation. We are only distracted from our vision by looking upon our conditions. This is why we must continue to seek out a fresh revelation from a contemporary God. The word of God removes scales off our eyes which enables us to become more like what we were designed to be.

There is a correlation between what we believe in our hearts and what we say out of our mouths. You cannot talk right out of your mouth if you are not filled with righteousness in your heart. With the heart man believeth unto Righteousness. Confession is made unto salvation. You have to think right in order to speak the language of the kingdom. Every kingdom has a specific language that must be verbalized in order to become a citizen. When your heart gets full of anything, it explodes through the mouth. People who don't know how to express themselves generally have nervous breakdowns. The pressure becomes unbearable until they implode. Out of the abundance of the heart, the mouth speaks.

There is a rest in God that will cause all worries to cease. Baptism in Christ draws a line in the sand for our past sins. There is a place in Him where we can have sweat less victories. Once we enter into a certain dimension of faith, things that use to bother us will not have the same effect anymore. Here we have to fight away anyone that may pull us out of this rest.

The attack on Pearl Harbor happened on December 7, 1941. It was the trigger that brought America into World War II. It was a surprise raid that killed 2,400 Americans. At least 2,985 people were killed in the September 11, 2001 terrorist attacks. Here in Charlotte, NC, we have experienced 77 homicides just this year alone in 2008. This city is 2nd behind New Orleans, LA, for the most murders committed in the United States. On the local news, a recession has finally been announced publicly for the 1st time. However, according to news sources, the start date of this recession is 1 year ago in December 2007. This is when the economy increased along with a severe decrease in national employment. For the first time in political history, a black man was elected as the 44th President. On February 17, 2009, analog signals will no longer work on standard televisions due to the evolution of digital technology. We even saw how gas prices skyrocketed up to almost $4.00 per gallon. These are truly the best of times and the worst of times. The world has experienced these types of challenges before. Some made it and some did not. The word of God empowers us to live above these situations. Pure faith comes from discipline, a renewed mind, and fellowship with God. We have to monitor what we hear, see, and even our thoughts. The bible says that a little leaven can leaven the whole loaf. It only takes a small amount of disbelief to water a negative seed (thought). Pure faith causes you to be delivered from every situation. Any question of God's will concerning anything that He has already promised and provided is just an excuse of unbelief.

When we go through earthquakes, storms, shakings, breakings, explosions, and pestilence, it is a sign. As it is in the natural, so shall it be in the spiritual. It is a sign that we are closer in these days than ever before to the providence that was pre-destined for our lives. It is not about what we are going through. Instead, it more important to focus on what you are traveling in. God has designed us to rest in the peace beyond all understanding that He has provided for us. This Peace is strong enough to fortify us. We are to rest in it regardless of what we are going through. He gives us courage in a crisis. Are you resting in the Peace of God? We must move forward while simultaneously remaining in His will. Don't look down and get discouraged for it only a trick of the enemy. Look upward from whence cometh our help. This is the time of hunger and it is imperative to come to God now. Our hunger provokes God to perform miracles in our life.

No matter how vehement the storms of life may become, it cannot beat its way through the believer who has submitted himself to the way of the Lord. Obeying the mandates of the Holy Spirit is our protection. He (Holy Spirit) will show us of things to come. The revelation of Holy Spirit launches the spirit of new beginnings in our lives. Everyday could possibly hold the promise of something new. The bible says that our latter days will be greater than our former days. This is my season of correction. Matthew 24:13 says, "[13]But he that shall endure unto the end, the same shall be saved." This race is not given to the swift or the faint at heart. It will only be won by ones who can endure hardness as a soldier. During the time of correction, everything that can be shaken will be shaken; so that those things that will not be shaken will remain.

CHAPTER 6: Delivered but Damaged

Romans 8:28

[28]We are assured and know that [God being a partner in their labor] all things work together and are [fitting into a plan] for good to and for those who love God and are called according to [His] design and purpose. (AMP)

The storms of life cause us to see God like never before. There is a Godly presence in the midst of the storm that we have never seen. There is something about a midnight experience that causes us to seek God. He encourages us to be of good cheer through His presence. In Greek, cheer means to "take courage". Jehovah Sharma means "God is present." When God proves that He is present we should immediately rest in His presence. It is evidence of an impending victory. If He be for us who can be against us? (Romans 8:31) There isn't a disorder, tumor, cancer, emotional disturbance, boss, job, credit union, credit report, company, hex, allegiance, curse, demon, wizard, soothsayer, astrologist, or any other thing that can be against us in His presence. Wherever we find His presence is also where His provisions are. You can be in the desert with no water. When He shows up, He will provide the water to quench our thirst. At our lowest point, God can change our situation through His presence. He only needs to speak one word to turn our midnight experience into an exhilarating sunrise.

I woke up at 3:36 am this morning and started driving to Charleston, SC to my client's site. On my way, I was listening to Bishop T. D. Jakes. However, I was led to turn it off for a moment of silence. In the still of the early morning darkness, I was captivated by a startling childhood remembrance. I received revelation about the entrance of the succubus spirit into my life. It is originally believed to be a female demon thought to have sexual intercourse with sleeping men. Webster's dictionary defines it as a demon assuming female form to have sexual intercourse with men in their sleep. Its counterpart is known as incubus. Webster defines the incubus spirit as an evil spirit that lies on persons in their sleep; one that has sexual intercourse with women while they are sleeping. It is further described as one that oppresses or burdens like a nightmare. This spirit is released through books, dreams, videos, sexual knowledge, and masturbation. The plural form is succubi which references multiple attacks generally during childhood. I have had to deal with the struggle of sexual perversion since I was in grade school. Although I have never had a desire to lay with men, I have always lusted after the flesh of women. I now understand why I have struggled with the desire to conquer so many women. If you have encountered these demons, DELIVERANCE and Spiritual Warfare can stop it!

The agony of the truth of this situation felt like when I smoked my first and only "wet daddy" (aka - a marijuana joint laced with sprinkles of cocaine). During my college years, I frequently smoked cannabis sativa to get high. Only this time, it was a "heart-stopping" event. The year was 1990. I received a "gift" from a friend. So we stepped outside to fire it up. My roommate, who no longer smoked pot, kept saying, "Hey man, there's something in there." I responded with "there's nothing in here." But he kept on saying it over and over again. He said, "I can smell it." Of course I could not smell it and kept on smoking anyway. A few minutes later I was barely able to breathe. I could actually feel my heart slowing down. My roommate then drove us back to our apartment. As we turned down our street to get to our apartment, we saw the flashing lights of a police car behind us. We were stopped by two Caucasian police officers who harassed us for several minutes. Although it only lasted a few minutes, it seemed to last forever. The lead officer's only explanation was, "I didn't like the way you guys took that last turn." My roommate was furious with me. But I was grateful for him. He had taken my car keys just before I cranked the car to drive us home. Can you say Grace, Favor, and Mercy of God?

That night is one that I have held secretly in my heart for many years. It is intrinsic to understand that every human being walking with two legs has many secrets. This is a fundamental commonality between us. Each individual has things, people, situations, circumstances, or information that we wish no one would ever know. This has a direct affect on our faith. Based on what I have seen, it is obvious that God wants to use our stinky stuff to set the captive free. When Lazarus died, there were those who were angry at Jesus for coming late. Though his physical body was dead, Jesus was confident that He had enough power to revive Lazarus. Jesus was also aware of the lack of faith surrounding the people who loved Lazarus. So, through the confidence that He carried, He walked into the house and raised Lazarus from the dead. This was a profound moment because He was able to introduce a new level of faith to those who witnessed this event. Only someone who is delivered from the strongholds of life can walk in this kind of power.

There is an old saying in the church, "Everybody that is saved is not delivered." What does this mean? A simple explanation is that many people have submitted to live under Jesus Christ as our Lord and personal savior. However, it does not mean that you are free from sin. Nor does it mean that you are free from struggles in life. It simply means that you are covered by salvation. Salvation is free and provides a shield over our lives. This can only come from a relationship with Jesus Christ. In the bible, it says that no weapon formed against us will prosper. That does not mean that the weapon will not be formed. It is imperative that we study the word of God in order to face the challenges of life. Life all by itself is a confrontational journey. Living in righteousness is easier said than done. In the Old Testament, righteousness was obtained by works. In Romans 3:22-23, righteousness is obtained through faith. God has placed His grace upon our lives so that we can carry His righteousness. We become the righteousness of God when we become saved and declare Jesus as our savior. All have sinned and come short of the glory of God. When we are born, sin is available to all. But, when we get saved, now righteousness is available unto all. The choice is up to you.

The ability to obtain righteousness is even more difficult when you have strongholds that prevent you from progressing in today's society. There are too many to name them all here. Some of the more fatal strongholds include bitterness, hatred, un-forgiveness, pride, fornication, drugs, cheating, stealing, lying, deception, lust, conspiracy, masturbation, jealousy, and envy. I call these the "Intangible 15." I chose these 15 strongholds because they can all be accomplished without ever getting exposed to the general public. A stronghold is anything that prevents us from being productive. They truly only occur in the mind because that is the battlefield. Victories are won or lost in the mind and then played out in the natural. In your lifetime, you will probably see a Christian fall. However, be careful to watch over your own salvation. The "Intangible 15" can exist in anyone at anytime about anything.

Oppressed people seem to spend out of the poverty of their situation. Simply put, they put effort into being oppressed. They sit around and think about being miserable with no hope of a brighter tomorrow.

They come to a place where it seems that they simply just can't move on. Do we really understand deliverance? Hebrews 6:1-3 describes the importance of moving forward in life by laying aside every weight. There is an apparent danger in not moving forward. Once we encounter this knowledge, it is important that we place it into action. Likewise, we must also be prepared for the criticism that is attached to it. We often feel the need to defend ourselves when others tell us that we have changed. Sometimes they even say it in a condescending manner. It is no longer necessary to defend yourself if you are a progressive person in God. For this cause alone, you will change because the wisdom of God is infinite. Otherwise, we will remain stagnant. Stagnant water draws gnats. Our lives should be like a gushing well springing forth with newness of life. Deliverance is a never-ending process. This process is a series of retroactive events that take place to reconcile our spirit with God's original plan. Although the timing may appear to be slow and sluggish, the fact that you have any movement at all is the most important element. Remember this one simple truth: ***Slow Steps Beat No Steps!***

This message is like a balm that provides therapy to my soul (mind, will, and emotions). It gets down into the pores of my personality and causes me to experience liberty. There is freedom that comes along with the sharing of individual triumphs. God has given me a vision for Praise and Worship Music Ministry. My mission is to fulfill the vision to the best of my ability. As the perception of my vision clears, the dependency on others begins to diminish. God already knew about my limitations before He called me. He knows that His grace is sufficient for my circumstances. In Mark 8:22-25, the blind man's vision gets clearer as he moves out of his homeland. He was led out because he had to learn to trust in the hope of trying something different. He felt like he had nothing to lose. At this point, he is open to the possibility of improvement. He was willing to be led. Sometimes we are just going on faith. Although I am delivered but damaged, I am not afraid to continue to be led by the Holy Spirit. It took three different touches for this man to see clearly. It was a process that he was willing to endure. Surrounding yourself with people of clear vision helps us to evaluate our current position. When we see our world clearly, only then can we change it effectively. Remember: you cannot change what you cannot see!

I used to believe that the number 13 meant bad luck. Then I was taught that life is not about luck at all. It's really about L.U.C.K. Living under Christ the King. Whether you are working for Him or against Him, we are all living under Christ the King. Deliverance can ONLY come from trusting in the anointing available through relationship with Jesus Christ. God will deliver us from the wilderness of our low expectations. There are four critical factors involved once you have been delivered from a stronghold, problem, or issue. They include the following:

1.   Forgive yourself and believe that deliverance belongs to you.
2.   Stay positive to maintain your deliverance.
3.   Establish relationships with positive people.
4.   Share your Testimony – it could help someone else.

We sometimes fail to realize that our trials are not really for us. Trials come to make us strong. However, we have to overcome them in order for God to get some Glory out of it. The glory is in your story to others who are struggling in the same area. God places you in the vanguard position to reveal His power. He places His anointing in us. Anointing is the "yoke-destroying" and "burden-removing" power given to us to conquer every situation in our life.

Change is the only constant in life. We must stop being faithful to dead situations. Eventually we process it as a loss or unfaithfulness. There is a time to die, a time to cry, a time to hold your peace, and a time to stretch forth. Let's not glorify the good ole' days. Rather let's celebrate the times that we are in right now. Success is predicated on what we are supposed to do during a season. The pain of our past is a payoff for the future. The compounded sum of good and bad experiences equips us for the progressiveness of the days that are to come. Vision without action only passes time. Yet, vision with action redefines your world.

God views each of us covered by Salvation. He gives us new mercies everyday. We are like Pearls in His eyes. Like humans, pearls are made up of 3 parts that include an upper shell, lower shell, and a ligament. They are comprised of accumulated dirt that is properly formed over a long period of time.

Humans are known as Triune Beings. We are the only creatures that can exist in both Heaven and Earth. We are a Spirit with a Soul that lives in a Body. We also accumulate dirt in our lives. These "dirty experiences" include divorce, layoffs, repossessions, rape, theft, lies, cheating, un-forgiveness, violence, foreclosures, marital problems, drugs, alcohol, financial struggles, emotional stress, personal sacrifices, and children out of wedlock. The satanic forces of this world use these dirty experiences in an attempt to discourage us from living in the joy of the Lord.

Every encounter will be used by God to give Him the glory. Because we are imperfect, we will forever be dependent upon Him. There are no perfect people in this world. So often, we look to the Saints of God to be perfect. Yet, none of us are perfect. We don't know of anyone who is perfect. Therefore, we should not judge others based on their actions. To some degree, we are all "delivered but damaged." U.P.S. packages are delivered daily. Sometimes the package is damaged when it arrives. This does not make it unusable. Although the box may be cracked, busted, or smashed, we eagerly inspect it to verify the condition of its contents.

Life is the same way. We go through various lessons in life that either makes us bitter or better. The key to enjoying life is to find the good in all situations. Joy can only come from God because it is a fruit of the spirit. Along the way, we may even enjoy some happiness. Happiness is a temporary emotion that causes us to take pleasure in the good moments of our existence here on Earth.

I now understand why this has all occurred. God allowed it to happen that He would get the glory out of this. The revelation that I have received is simple. The place of your greatest misery is going to be the place of your greatest ministry! God wants to get in our business by using our stinky stuff. There is a portion of our life that we have reserved only for ourselves. We refuse to share our most intimate embarrassing moments. Those private mistakes that show what we used to be are awkward. They create uncomfortable conversation when shared with the general public. This is even after being delivered from the action in question. Yet it is liberating to tell the truth about your past and share your shortcomings with others.

Although I am delivered but damaged, my life is not beyond repair. I am a living witness that God can take your test and convert it into a testimony. God can use your mistakes to transform the lives of others. He can hold us in His hands as a broken vessel for years. In the twinkling of an eye, He can transform us into whatever He so desires. What can we do with a child, marriage, or career that is flawed? God makes it new again from items that are already in place. He used the same vessel (person) with a flaw or shortcoming. Although it was messed up, He can transform that same vessel into someone new. It seems as though you would want to throw away the flawed ingredients and start over. This is the power of God's Grace. He did not make another vessel. He is the potter and we are the clay.

CHAPTER 7: Same old world, New Perspective

The Whole Armor of God!

- Helmet of Salvation
- Breastplate of Righteousness
- Shield of Faith
- Belt of Truth
- Sword of the Spirit (God's word)
- Shoes to spread the gospel of Peace

Ephesians 6:11

[11]Put on God's whole armor [the armor of a heavy-armed soldier which God supplies], that you may be able successfully to stand up against [all] the strategies and the deceits of the devil. (AMP)

I was sitting in my hotel room watching Trinity Broadcast Network. All of a sudden an astonishing thought entered my mind. When I put on the girdle of truth, it gives me integrity. When I stand behind the breastplate of righteousness, it gives me confidence. When I march with feet shod in the preparation of God's peace, I experience sweatless victories. As I carry the shield of faith, I have no fear of the pestilence that surrounds me. When I wear the helmet of salvation, I am covered from evil. When I carry the sword of the spirit, I am equipped for every situation. This is what is meant by Romans 8:31 where it reads, "31What shall we then say to these things? If God be for us, who can be against us?" (KJV). The revelation that I received while sitting in my hotel room that night was simply this. When we put on the full armor of God our Father, then we began to look just like Him. Therefore, the devil no longer recognizes us as the struggling saint who is still trying to get it together. He can only see God at that point. It is a known fact that we are Triune beings who can exist in heaven as well as in the earth. However, we don't walk around in the spirit 24 hours per day. But, at the times that we do, we look like our Father to the devil. During these moments we become somewhat invincible and cause the enemy to flee.

My biggest pet peeve is Christians in the corporate world who are afraid to share their testimonies. I get so tired of those professional Christians. They are happy go lucky, proper talking, briefcase carrying, wing tip shoe wearing, name brand only, country club membership card carrying folk who don't know God between the hours of 9am and 5pm. While it not necessary to preach a sermon in the boardroom, it is essential that others know that side of you. Some people will never read a bible. But they will read you, the living epistle of God. That's why we must submit ourselves Holy and acceptable to Him. A Christian lifestyle is important to non-Christians. Whether they admit it or not, they are constantly watching your actions. You build your confidence in God by saying what God says about you. But you must say it with your mouth. Even if you feel stupid saying it, you must say it all the time. Say it until you get it in your heart, and you'll become so confident in God that you acknowledge Him everywhere you go, no matter where you are.

I am now a firm believer that God can use you wherever you are. But you must be where He tells you to go. I have also learned that my previous overeating in the natural was in direct relation to my hunger for God. If applied properly, the following eight strategies will GUARANTEE a more successful life:

1. Spend time with God before making major decisions (ask for His guidance).
2. Follow His directions without changing the instructions received. (focus)
3. Don't allow someone else's bad attitude to steal your joy. (remain cheerful)
4. Get into your rightful position (stop being distracted).
5. Work hard and play hard. (learn to balance employment, family time, and vacations)
6. Read the bible and pray without ceasing! (study to be approved before God and men)
7. Understand that God's presence is Protection. (Allow Him do the heavy lifting in life)
8. Be consistent. (Don't procrastinate or make excuses.)

Life is a series of moments. We should all keep a time capsule. This is simply a box of memories. It contains pictures, newspaper clippings, diagrams, letters, dvd's, cd's and any other items that we desire to preserve. There are times of crisis, instances of mourning, occasions of defeat, periods of agony, stages of preparation, transitional phases, flashes of greatness, eras of joy, cycles of drama, intervals of victory, and moments of perfection! It sounds like we should be covered from head to toe with full body armor. God has provided a complete covering for us as Believers so that we are protected in areas of weakness.

For we wrestle not against flesh and blood, but against principalities (chiefs) against powers (authorities) against the (world) rulers of the darkness (obscurity) of this world (age or time) against spiritual (supernatural) wickedness (malicious hurtfulness) in high places (above the sky). (Ephesians 6:12) This is the hierarchy of the devil and all his lower level devils and demons. From his perspective, he is the god of this world and has a pecking order of intelligent princes and mindless grunts to do his works of oppression (influence, depression, oppression, obsession and possession). Remember to put this armor on each and every day, and like the credit card commercial says, don't leave home without it! We are now living in days where most people only feel safe when they are carrying a gun around.

Harrold, Texas is a tiny Texas school district that has commanded national attention. Trustees at the Harrold Independent School District approved a district policy change in October 2007 so employees can carry concealed firearms to deter and protect against school shootings, provided the gun-toting teachers follow certain requirements. †Since the 911 terrorist attacks, there is a resurgence of vulnerability for employees and residents across this country. There has never in life been a time that warrants the protection of God more than right now.

Psalms 91:4 reads, "He shall cover thee with his feathers and under his wings shalt thou trust, his truth shall be thy shield and buckler." (KJV) He is the only one who can keep you safe from ALL danger. I have always believed that there is nothing wrong with having a gun at home. Some people are horrified at having a gun at home. But you have to understand that even if you have a gun; it still may not save you. If a burglar wants to get to you, they may get you before you can get to the gun. Therefore, you have to have something beyond the physical protection of a weapon. The others may say, "Well, if you are a true person of faith, then there is no need for weapons." My only question to those people is, "Do you have a lock on your doors?" Of course you do. But, as bad as times are now, you have to trust in God to side step the traps of the enemy. Life has the power to make you feel like giving up.

Silence can sometimes be described as Golden. However, the wrong type of silence can be fatal. The silence of men has helped to lead to the decay of the family structure. The fabric of today's society is predicated upon the concept of a stabilized family infrastructure. More households are now being led by women than ever before. The statistics are startling. In the United States, the 2000 census showed that 24.8 million, or nearly 24 percent of the nation's 105.5 million households, were the traditional home with married parents and children. By comparison, 9.8 million households, or 9 percent of all

U.S. households, were headed by a man or woman raising a child alone or without a spouse living at home. † Even with stats like these, God is causing a shift in the atmosphere. Men are now being forced back into the vanguard position of the family unit. This is what God Himself intended for us. We are the best counselors, teachers, providers, and builders who should complimented through a covenant marriage with a woman as prescribed by the word of God. Maybe we didn't get it right the first time, or the second time, or the third time, or the fourth time. Conversely, it should not deter us from our duties and responsibilities as the head of household. Prime time comedian Steve Harvey says it best, "If you don't understand the joy and beauty of marriage and family in this lifetime, you have missed the boat."

Although the world around us may never seem to change, we are still required to hold ourselves to a higher standard. For years now, I have been traveling in a never-ending circle of unconsciousness. I have wasted countless hours outside of the will of God for my life. He is trying to use my problems to Direct, Inspect, Correct, Protect, and Perfect me. The problems that I face will either crush me or cultivate me. From an individual perspective, success can be measured in lessons learned. Life is a series of moments. It is my sincere desire to positively touch a multitude of lives along the way.

I believe that one essential element is following the teachings of the bible. Half of the people we know don't even try to read it. Yet, we have to swear by it before ever speaking a word of testimony in a court case before a judge.

How do you put on the whole armor of God? Love is the belt that ties it all together. The decision to love is where you start. Mature Christians understand that Love is a weapon. Have you ever heard the term "Love your enemies to death?" My mother was a perfect example. I couldn't understand for the life of me why she was so nice to people who despised her, spread untruths about her, and didn't even acknowledge her presence at certain times. That's the true love of Jesus Christ! That is hard to do. Only a mature Christian can put on the whole armor of God.

CHAPTER 8: Never give up!

2 Corinthians 4:16

¹⁶Therefore we do not become discouraged (utterly spiritless, exhausted, and wearied out through fear). Though our outer man is [progressively] decaying and wasting away, yet our inner self is being [progressively] renewed day after day. (AMP)

There is no action that takes place except that it is first preceded by a conscious thought. The most amazing products aren't born from metal, wood, or plastic. They're born from human ideas. No matter how valuable the products and services that exist in a business, the true worth lies with its people, their imagination, creativity, and mind power. And by learning how to harness your God-given intellectual and imaginative abilities, you have the ability to become a millionaire, catapult your business, and even change the world.

Thoughts of Success and failure enter through same passageway. There are times in our lives when the thought of giving up seems to outweigh every other thought. We feel as though there is no hope left. We appear to be in a spiral breakdown destined for doom. Secretly, in our heart of hearts, we have already given up. The rest of the world just doesn't know about it yet. So we go to work each day, go to church each week, attend the ball games, pass through the grocery store, and even go to parties. But, secretly, in our heart, the situation that is currently pressing us has beaten us into submission. This is why we no longer talk about among friends or relatives. In our mind, some things should just be left alone. For instance, I no longer talk about my divorce, my ex-fiancee's infidelity, my conspiracy to commit murder, items that were stolen from me, things I have stolen, lies that I used to tell, sleeping with married women, and other activities never told. Yet, I have developed a faith to move beyond them all. I never even thought that God would forgive from some of this stuff. Yes, even me, a faith-filled, tongue-talking, strong-walking, anointed preaching, and devoted believer in God. Even I had doubts that He would forgive me because I was Nast to the Tee (aka downright Nasty!). That's why when I preach in the local prisons here, I used to feel like I am no better than any of them simply because of my past indiscretions. The process of rededicating my life to the church has challenged my faith to no end.

When people who knew me before now find out that I am ministering, they are shocked. It only validates the old adage, "The preachers used to be the worst ones." In my case, it is certainly true. There are times when I feel so frail that it is as if I have been dominated by my past. If I could turn back the hands of time, I would do so many things differently. Time is our most precious commodity. Once it is gone, you never get it back. So now, I can only pick from where I am. No matter the condition or consequence of my past, I have to progress forward in life and not become paralyzed out of fear of my wrongdoings. Romans 8:26 describes to us the job of the Holy Spirit. The Spirit itself maketh intercession for us with groanings which cannot be uttered. The Holy Spirit is here to help us. We have help where we are weak. We have help where we can't get the job done. And the help that we have is the Holy Ghost. But notice that you can only be helped when you are doing something. If you are not doing anything, then you don't need help to do nothing. So we can see that it does not say that the Holy Spirit does everything for us. However, it does say that He helps our infirmities.

Although I have grown considerably in the past several months, I am still humbled by God's grace in my life. The only thing that I really have in life is Faith. I constantly rely on Holy Spirit to help me in the faith department. We know that without faith, it is impossible to please God. Also, faith without works is dead. Faith is never truly established until we begin the process of surrendering our will to God's will. This is what occurs as a result of getting saved.

In order to be saved, you ONLY have to recite Romans 10:9-10. God gave authority in the earth to man. You received that authority when you were born again; and you do not have to get rid of all the imperfections in your life first before you activate that authority. However, you still have to challenge yourself to become a better person.

Romans 12:3 says "For I say, through the grace given unto me, to every man that is among you, not to think of himself more highly than he ought to think; but to think soberly, according as God hath dealt to every man the measure of faith." God's word has the power to provoke a change in every person. It keeps us from getting the big head syndrome, which is typically fostered by arrogance. What's putting you over is that God has blessed you in spite of yourself. Somebody who has gone on before you prayed for you to be blessed. Some of us had mothers, grandmothers and great-grandmothers that prayed for God's mercy to be extended toward us. Some of us are still living off the prayers and blessings of great-grandparents that we have never even met. This is why I am humbled to the point of change. It makes me grateful that God thought enough of me to touch me like this. Only God gets the glory for all the good in your life. God is good all the time. I was listening to another minister and he said, "You don't really believe in miracles until you need one!" Immediately, I thought to myself about the truthfulness of this statement.

We give tithes and offerings out of faith. It is a system of circulation. God gives seed to the sower. It represents the law of reciprocity. Even though all that we have belongs to God, we are faithful that this provides protection because of our obedience. We should always seek divine direction by bringing our finances under God's protection. Money is not evil. We should never worship the gift over the giver. The future of our finances is secure from the devourer based on these concepts. Bishop T. D. Jakes teaches that business owners should pay tithes based upon the type of business you have. If it is a sole proprietorship or S Corporation, then you should pay tithes on the profit. The profit margin becomes your personal income. If it is a C Corporation with employees, then you tithe on income made after the overhead has been taken care of. The monies that remain are your profit.

God has authority over our losses, debt, financial curses, and bad investments. He does not want us to invest in depreciating property. He will protect us from doing the right thing at the wrong time. He will increase our discernment to understand which season we are in. This is called the art of waiting for the right moment. He will even enhance our reputation, image, and lifestyle. People will see the blessings on our lives. The blessings cannot be hidden and will overflow in our natural existence. In other words, people will look at you and see prosperity on you.

God opens up a channel based on tithing and offerings. It is not what we say that opens up the Heavens. It is what you do. Obedience opens up the Heavens. God will dispense what He has withheld. Even the cross was an offering as talked about in Hebrews 9:14, 28; 10:12; 11:17. This is why the grave could not hold Jesus because His death was an offering to God. For this cause, God will give us access to excess. His name is El Shaddai, which means more than enough.

In the Christian church, we teach that salvation is free. On one hand, it does not cost anything to speak the kingship of Jesus Christ over our lives to be saved. On the other hand, it cost God the life of His only Son. When we began to live through Him, it's eventually going to cost us something too. Therefore, it is incumbent that we understand something about the price of salvation. The princes of darkness are well aware of who we are when we accept Jesus as our Lord and personal Savior. These satanic forces have one mission. They want to keep us from ever getting to that place of understanding of the true will of God for our lives.

Trials come to make us strong. This is when faith wells up on the inside. God has to show up periodically in our lives to prevent us from losing faith in Him. This statement almost sounds contradictory to the previous paragraph. However, put yourself in the hot seat for a moment. Has anything ever happened to you that caused you to wonder, "Where is God in all of this?" And then, He brought you out of it to the other side. Some time may have passed in your life. But eventually, you come to yet another big challenge. Only this time, it seems bigger than the last one. To complicate matters, this one is not even attached in any way, shape, form, or fashion to the previous test. This is actually something totally different. So, once again, you have to call on the Master for help. What if He didn't show up for a very long time in this new thing? The human side of us will begin to wonder, "Where is God?" The spiritual side, when it is receiving the right food or input, will go to war with the flesh. God will turn your pain into power when we pierce through the veil of the flesh. We have to fight for freedom from the bondage of our fleshly nature. Freedom is the heritage of the believer. Truth is the light of this freedom. Truth is not designed to keep you from sin. Sin from the 1800's is the same as sin in 2007. Look for scriptures that crucify your flesh. The truth of God's word was created to set you free.

Our spirit man will fight on our behalf by speaking positive affirmations to you and through you. This is why we must renew our minds daily. Problems, tests, and trials come daily to make us strong. The ironic part of this is that they are not even for us. They are allowed by God so that He might get the glory out of every situation.

These experiences then become transformed into testimonies to help others realize the power of the Almighty!

What have I learned from all of these experiences? It is quite possible to be knowledgeable, have wisdom, and even understanding of the word. Yet, I have lived for many years with this understanding without properly applying it in every area of my life. I have only applied it in my life to certain areas as needed for a season. Now I have a spiritual mandate to apply God's word in my life lest I faint from the exhaustion of my past indiscretions. Don't make the same mistake as I have. If you do, you travel in circles around things that you should glide over without breaking a sweat. Take the truth of God and hold it close like a little baby. Nurture it as if your very life depends on it. Only then will you be successful through Him.

Once we come into the full knowledge of what we are in Him, the devil's power is severed once and for all. It's like riding a bicycle. At some point, we must make up in our minds that we are going to ride without the training wheels. It is all about balance. Everything in life has a balance point. Once you find it, you must operate in that balance in order to have a successful livelihood. I understand that there were bumps and bruises from previous rides. However, it's just life! When we finally take off the training wheels of life, we can progressively move without the assistance of others. We can strive forward in the anointing power which releases us from the bondage of strongholds. It has "yoke-destroying" and "burden-removing" authority which launches us into a new level of liberty through the Grace of almighty God. We are no longer O.O.C. (aka Out of Control). It is now time to live large and be in charge. This is accomplished by being fully persuaded that nothing shall separate me from the love of God which is in Christ Jesus (Romans 8:38). If you ever allow this one bible verse to resonate deep within your spirit, you will ultimately give the powers of darkness a spiritual headache. They will flee from you like roaches with cerebral palsy under the affects of ultra-strength Raid. You will literally amputate their orchestrated campaigns against you.

Jesus took from Satan the keys of death, hell and the grave. We read in Hebrews chapter 2 that we no longer have to fear death. It said Satan had (past tense) the power of death. He doesn't have the power `of death anymore. It has been taken from him. If he could have done away with you he would have done it by now. But he could not.

For this reason alone, we should have faith. We are covered from head to toe and protected from death. Faith, which is the opposite of fear, now becomes a powerful force in our lives. Faith comes when fear has been removed. We generally try all other options before trying faith. Sometimes it is due to curiosity, pride, or emotion. In the long run, faith becomes the only option left. Faith seems to work when it is the only option. Of course, it should be the first option. But let's be real! We don't always choose it first. But when we do, it never fails.

Conclusion: Offer of Salvation

Ephesians 2:8-9

"[8]For by grace you have been saved through faith. And this is not your own doing; it is the gift of God, [9]not a result of works, so that no one may boast." (ESV – English Standard Bible)

Right now, I am calling out to God on behalf of every man and woman who wants to experience a new life. I stand naked, unashamed, and readily equipped to lead others to Christ. I intercede on your behalf right now. This is an opportunity for me to request God's help in your situation. God will change your direction. By grace and through faith you will be changed. This moment is for those of you who have never accepted Jesus as your Lord and personal Savior. Also, if you are already saved and would like to rededicate your life to the mission of God, then this chapter is for you as well. In Romans 10:9-10, it reads, "[9]Because if you acknowledge and confess with your lips that Jesus is Lord and in your heart believe (adhere to, trust in, and rely on the truth) that God raised Him from the dead, you will be saved. [10]For with the heart a person believes (adheres to, trusts in, and relies on Christ) and so is justified (declared righteous, acceptable to God), and with the mouth he confesses (declares openly and speaks out freely his faith) and confirms [his] salvation."

We are saved from the penalty of sin, but not from the power of sin. You have to get to a place where you say, "Not my will, but Thy will be done." Sometimes you have to say this over and over again. Let it get down into you soul. Write these words on the tablet of your heart. Meditate and trust in them. Only then can you receive the benefit of what it means to truly be free in Christ. Would you like to rededicate your life or be saved today along with me? If the answer is yes, then pray this simple prayer with me.

"Heavenly Father,
I realize that I have not become everything that You originally designed me to be. But, right now, I apologize for all of my sins, known and unknown. Jesus, come and live in me. I declare that Jesus died on the cross for my sins and that God has raised Him from the dead. I make You the Lord over my life once and for all. By faith, I declare that I am Saved, in the Mighty name of Jesus! Amen!"

If you prayed this simple prayer, then tell me about it. I want to stay in contact with you through electronic email or postal mail. I have information that can assist you in daily living. Feel free to write me. Tell me the good news. Please go to my ministry contact page which is located at http://www.savedandserving.org/salvation.html. Select submit your feedback. Include your contact information. I will send materials that will assist you in your Christian walk. Find a good local church that focuses on praise & worship. Hopefully, it will be near your home so that you may continue to grow in the word of God. My struggles are lessened more and more as I read the word of God. As we go deeper in God's word, we are no longer struggling with the devil. He is now struggling with us. God has broken into my life through revelation. My life was invaded by the holiness of His salvation. Salvation is eternal life and once exciting fleeting moments are no longer able to govern me like before. I hope that my horrifying past has helped someone look beyond the darkness and into brighter days. Be encouraged to receive more of His spirit in your life. It is my prayer that God continue to bless you. I love you and thank you for supporting my ministry – which is truly a vision from God. If He can use me, He can use anybody. I am a living witness.

Reference and Online Resources

1.   Ministry of Deliverance - www.RefugeRanchMinistries.net. †
2.   Statistics from http://www.fww.org/famnews/single-parents.html †
3.   Statistics from http://www.whitings-writings.com/diatribes/strange_fruit.htm †
4.   Statistics from http://library.thinkquest.org/12111/mculley.html †
5.   The Holy Bible (King James Version) - KJV
6.   The Holy Bible (Amplified Version) - AMP
7.   The Holy Bible (New Living Translation) – NLT
8.   The Holy Bible (English Standard Bible) - ESV
9.   Images taken from http://www.reverendfun.com ♪
10.   Images taken from http://www.johncoulthart.com ♪
11.   Images taken from http://www.plotinus.com ♪
12.   Images taken from http://logobrand.com/art_gallery.shtml ♪
13.   Images taken from http://www.tgm.org/ ♪
14.   Images taken from http://www.foundationsforfreedom.net ♪
15.   Images taken from http://www.floridaqgunworks.com ♪
16.   Images taken from http://www.thelightanddarkseries.com ♪
17.   Images taken from http://www.stickerart.com.au/ ♪
18.   Images taken from www.woundedlamb.com) ♪
19.   Statistics from http://www.chron.com/disp/story.mpl/front/5945430.html †
20.   Story from http://www.nytimes.com/2008/08/12/us/12ohio.html

♪ - This symbol represents sources that have provided images for the current edition of "Bondage of Bitterness." The source of information is included in the above-listed references.

† - This symbol represents statistical references made within the contents of this book. The source of information is included in the above-listed references.

TO
GOD
BE
THE
GLORY!

www.ingramcontent.com/pod-product-compliance
Lightning Source LLC
Chambersburg PA
CBHW051706090426

42736CB00013B/2559